THE PROMISE OF VISION

CAUSING SUPERNATURAL GROWTH

BY
DR STUART ROBINSON

Author of best-selling books *Mosques & Miracles,*
Defying Death and *The Prayer of Obedience*

**CHI
BOOKS**

CHI
BOOKS

Published by CHI-Books
PO Box 6462,
Upper Mt Gravatt, QLD 4122, Australia

www.chibooks.org
resources@cityharvest.org.au

Copyright © 2006 by Stuart Robinson
Redesigned and printed in 2012 under CHI-Books imprint.
Print edition ISBN 978-0-9870891-7-5
eBook edition ISBN 978-0-9870891-8-2

Scripture quotations in this publication are from the *Holy Bible,* New International Version (NIV). Copyright © 1973, 1978, 1984 International Bible Society, Zondervan Bible Publishers.

Originally printed under CityHarvest Publications imprint.
ISBN 978-0-9775602-0-2

Printed in Australia, United Kingdom and the United States of America.

Distributed in the USA and Internationally by Ingram Book Group and Amazon.

Cover design: CHI-Books

Layout: Dave Gray / Jonathan Gould

About This Book

Nothing much of consequence results until we become serious about prayer. This is especially so in co-operating with God in his desire to grow church. But when a prayer base is established, what next?

As we search the scriptures, there are so many references and examples of what God wants to do within his church. However comparatively, so often little of that seems to be happening. In that situation it is common to rationalise God's promises down to explain or excuse our levelled ineffectiveness.

The better course would be, by faith to lift our expectations up to what God's Word declares should be so, to wait upon him for his vision for what he wants us to become and then to continue to wait upon him to discern how he wants us to proceed.

This book is about "vision", what it is, how we get it, what place it plays and how to implement it. It is a missing component in many Christian activities. May God reveal his vision for his work through you—as you read and continue to wait upon him.

'WHEN GOD GIVES A VISION,
TRANSACT BUSINESS ON
THAT LINE, NO MATTER
WHAT IT COSTS'

Oswald Chambers

To Allan and Val, Ian and Barbara, fellow visionaries,

who have kept me true to God's call and vision for us all.

CONTENTS

ONE

BACK TO THE FUTURE

When Steven Koski was visiting Disneyworld in Orlando, Florida, he said to his guide, "It's a pity Walt Disney didn't live to see this." The tour guide replied, "Oh, but he did. If he didn't first imagine it in his mind, believe wholeheartedly in his heart that it was possible and then develop that belief in others, it wouldn't be here."

Visionaries like Walt Disney, whether in commerce, science, industry, religion or any other field of human endeavour, in every era, are few and far between.

The prophecies of doomsdayers, nay-sayers, cynics and people with little vision and even less faith, are more the order of the day. If their pronouncements had happened few of us would be here.

In 1743 one M. Montesquieu declared that the population of the earth was decreasing every day and if this continued, in another ten centuries the earth would be nothing but desert. But if that happens probably it won't be through decreasing population. Twentieth century pundits considered it would be through overpopulation. In 1903 Henry Adams said that his calculations indicated that 1950 would be the year when the world "must go smash".

In 1968 Paul Erlich in his best selling book "The Population Bomb", predicted that in the 1970s, famine would be so wide spread that hundreds of millions of people would starve to death.

In 1972 no less a prestigious body than the Club of Rome, released a study concluding that the world would run out of gold by 1981, mercury by

1985, tin by 1987, zinc by 1990, petroleum by 1992 and copper, lead and gas by 1993.

None of those commodities have run out and we are still here – as are many false "prophets". They are unlikely to vanish quickly in spite of their long run of erroneous predictions.

In the seventeenth century advisors to the King and Queen of Spain were of the opinion that Columbus's voyages were unlikely to yield any good result. Even after the immense benefits of the New World were much better appreciated, vision was still in short supply. In a United States Senate speech in 1848, Daniel Webster said, "I have never heard of anything more ridiculous, more absurd and more affrontive to all sober judgment than the cry that we are profiting by the acquisition of New Mexico and California. I hold that they are not worth a dollar!"

Fortunately for many of us Dr Alfred Velpeau also got it wrong when he announced in 1839 that "the abolition of pain in surgery is a chimera. It is absurd to go on seeking it today. Knife and pain are two words in surgery that must forever be associated in the consciousness of the patient. To this compulsory combination we shall have to adjust ourselves."

If only Admiral William D. Leahy had been right we would have had far fewer international crises. He told President Truman in 1945 that the Atomic Bomb was "the biggest fool thing we have ever done. The bomb will never go off and I speak as an expert in explosives."

So much for trusting in "experts"! Not that he was alone in faulty vision.

In 1835 railroad "experts" dismissed as extremely improbable the development of any system of transport that could move at a speed exceeding 16 kms an hour. We do need to be generous however because predictions about technology have a long history of being wrong.

When a US east coast bishop visited a mid-western Christian religious college, he stayed at the home of the college president who also worked as professor of physics and chemistry. In an after dinner discussion the bishop declared that the "millennium" of which the Bible speaks, couldn't be far off because everything which could be invented had already been invented and all that could be known about nature had also been discovered. The college president disagreed. He was of the opinion that there would be many more discoveries. The somewhat dismissive bishop challenged the president to name just one such possibility. The president replied that he believed that within 50 years people would be able to fly. The bishop considered the proposal preposterous. He thought only angels were intended to fly.

Such was the visionary incapacity of Bishop Wright, whose two sons were Orville and Wilbur. Later, just one week before the Wright brothers' famous first flight on December 17 1903 at Kitty Hawk, North Carolina, the New York Times also ridiculed the idea that humans would ever fly.

Western Union pontificated that the telephone had too many shortcomings to be seriously considered as a means of communication and the device was therefore inherently of no value to them. Many parents would have wished they could have been right.

Visionless David Sarnoff stated that "the wireless music-box has no imaginable commercial value. Who would pay for a message sent to nobody in particular?" Who indeed? Only most of the world's entire population!

But in a competition for those who set themselves up as authorities who have least vision, perhaps the prize should be awarded to the writers of a certain car owner's manual, who in 1913 confidently stated, "The automobile has now developed to the point where it is not anticipated there will be further developments or changes and this manual should be a reliable guide for the motorist of the future." That could be so if one restricted oneself to driving only pre-1913 models.

Envisioning technological advance is obviously fraught with risk. Surely we couldn't make the same mistakes with weightier human activities such as religion? No?

> VISION, WHEN AUTHENTIC, IS SO POWERFUL IT CANNOT BE IGNORED BY US ALL SIMPLY BECAUSE OF INEPTITUDE OR ABUSE BY SOME.

In 1968 American sociologist Peter Berger said that by "the 21st century, religious believers are likely to be found only in small sects, huddled together to resist a worldwide secular culture." One shouldn't judge Berger too harshly. After all, this was in the decade in which God was declared dead – at least in Western thinking. The trouble was nobody told the rest of the world—or God for that matter.

Clearly to talk authoritatively about vision and the future invites scepticism if not ridicule, because of a well documented history of failure in the past in this area. But vision, when authentic, is so powerful it cannot be ignored by us all simply because of ineptitude or abuse by some.

One night in 1898 a little known Austrian Jewish newspaper reporter had what he described as a vision, complete with the audible fluttering of angels' wings. He was not particularly religious. He knew little of Biblical or Jewish history. His name was Theodor Herzl. Impelled by his vision he wrote a book telling Jews they must move from wherever they were, to reassemble in Palestine to form a Jewish state.

After completing his initial project Herzl wondered if he had not been insane to write as he had. After all, he was unknown and had neither money nor influence. But in time he would be admitted into the presence of kings, millionaires and to the hearts of millions of Jews scattered around the world.

Exactly 50 years later, in 1948, the State of Israel was re-established.

In that same year, another Jew who had become a Christian pastor, was kidnapped by Romanian Communist police. For the next 14 years he was often in solitary confinement, isolated and imprisoned 10 metres below ground. During that time God gave him a vision of an international mission to the Communist World, which he faithfully implemented for the rest of his life. His name was Richard Wurmbrand.

TWO

VISION - CONCEPT AND DEFINITION

In the Christian west, if practice is any indicator, vision is not highly regarded or keenly anticipated as a legitimate means of God directing his servants who in turn may lead churches, local or national. We have been so influenced by the previous century's dominance of rationalism, scientism, affluence and materialism as to disregard such a well attested Biblical methodology. In our Bible Colleges, Schools of Divinity or Theological departments in universities, we would be hard pressed to discover anywhere, even an introductory course on vision, though it is still testified as a means by which God commonly directs those of non-Western and non-Christian origin.

So what is this that eludes our experience?

Specifically it may mean an ecstatic experience by which new knowledge is divinely revealed through something which is seen. Old Testament prophets Isaiah, Jeremiah, Ezekiel and Daniel are but a few who record such experiences. In the New Testament there is Zacharias (Luke 1:23), Ananias (Acts 9:10), Peter (Acts 10:10), Paul (Acts 16:9) and many others.

In a more general sense in terms of ministry, George Barna, in his best selling book, "The Power of Vision", gives the most comprehensive definition of recent times.

He says,

Vision… is a clear mental image of a preferable future imparted by God to his chosen servants and is based upon an accurate understanding of God, self and circumstances.

Vision is not wishful thinking or unsubstantiated nebulous, abstract hope. It takes concrete, specific, distinct forms in response to contemporary spiritual needs and opportunities. It supplies an answer to the question of what God wants us to become and to do. It is a target which beckons us forward.

One might also add as with any other supernatural impartation, if it is of God, it will not be in contradiction to any previous revelation or teaching within the Bible, which actually gives quite a lot of help in understanding vision.

THREE

OLDEST FUTURISTIC BOOK

Christians are citizens of two worlds, that of the physical and time bound world which we currently inhabit and that of eternity beyond measurement. Our loyalty to the latter effects our operations in the former. The most reliable manual on how to operate in the present world in the light of our future habitation comes via the Bible, which through precept and example presents principles by which God operates.

> WHAT WOULD WE ATTEMPT FOR GOD IF WE KNEW WE COULDN'T FAIL AND FINANCES WERE NO BARRIER.

The apostle Paul said that God *"...is able to do immeasurably more than all we ask or imagine, according to his power that is at work within us."* (Ephesians 3:20) In practice, what that can mean is that if we dream up the greatest achievement we can think of for our lives in ministry through our respective churches, God can come up with something even bigger. That being so, then the question we need to ask is, what would we attempt for God if we knew we couldn't fail and finances were no barrier.

Vision originates with a word from God. The human component is faith to believe, implemented by submission and discipline to obey, even if what is suggested seems to our limited understanding, to be irrational. It's not a matter of wanting to walk on water, but whether or not we are willing to get out of the boat (Matthew 14:22-32).

God wants to demonstrate his supernatural abilities through us so that all the world might know that he exists (1 Samuel 17:45-47; 1 Kings 8:60).

Frequently his intentions may be thwarted because we make use of only a little boy's lunch, when he desires and is ready to feed 5000 others (John 6:1-15).

Consider Noah.

When he was over 500 years of age God instructed him to build a large boat of unprecedented proportions. We don't know if at the start of the enterprise, Noah had ever seen rain, a flood or even had tools, to do the job. As a farmer (Genesis 9:20) almost certainly he would have had neither knowledge nor experience in boat building. It wasn't until he was 600 years old that the task was complete and the 150 metre long boat was ready to be floated.

From a human perspective the whole process is summed up by the words, *"Noah did everything, just as God commanded him"* (Genesis 6:22).

God's command may have seemed unreasonable to the point of being almost unintelligible. Neighbours and passers by may have laughed at this backyard dry land project of many decades. Yet Noah, as a current footwear slogan urges - just did it.

The case of Abraham was even more bizarre (Genesis 12:1-3).

God gave him a vision of what his person and influence would be in the future. He was shown no sign posts or road maps. He was given no guarantees. But the vision was so compellingly powerful that Abraham left all his kinfolk, with all its securities and set off for what for him were totally new lands. For a tribally based society, this would have been unprecedented. It would still be almost unthinkable today in that part of the world.

Later God gave Abraham another vision reassuring him that God would implement that which was spoken earlier (Genesis 15:1-7). When Abraham was 99 years of age it was confirmed again (Genesis 17:1-8).

On yet a fourth occasion a heavenly delegation visited Abraham to reassure him that that which was divinely decreed many years earlier, would come to pass literally within the next 12 months. When Abraham was 100 years old and Sarah was 90, Isaac was born (Genesis 21:5). And it happened without any IVF intervention!

> IT WAS NORMATIVE FOR OLD TESTAMENT PROPHETS TO BE INSTRUCTED AND GUIDED THROUGH VISIONS.

When it came time to deliver God's people from slavery, to relocate them and to issue the law codes by which he expected them to live for all future generations, Moses was the one chosen (Exodus 3:1-10) to receive repeated callings and visions by way of instruction, through various means. Many recruitment experts would have considered him unfit for the assignment of initiating a rebellion and leading former shepherds and construction contract labourers for 40 years till they became a unified, significant fighting force, capable of carving out their own destiny at the expense of anyone who got in the way. Moses himself would have agreed with such an assessment (Exodus 4). But with a supernatural visitation, a vision was born which Moses followed for the rest of his life.

When Moses died, his leadership role was taken by his apprentice Joshua. Through another vision he also was commissioned to lead the occupation of Canaan, to initiate the process by which it would later become Israel (Joshua 1:1-9).

Nehemiah received his vision from God to rebuild the walls of Jerusalem while he was fasting and praying (Nehemiah 1:4; 2:12).

It was normative for Old Testament prophets to be instructed and guided through visions to enable them to make interpretative pronouncements about the times in which they lived as well as the future of nations (Isaiah 1:1; 6:1-13; Jeremiah 1:1ff; Ezekiel 1:1ff; Obadiah 1:1ff; Habakkuk 2:2-20).

Joel foresaw a time when God's spirit would be poured out on all people. One of the effects of this would be many would see visions (Joel 2:28).

In the New Testament era, the Apostle Peter confirmed that the new age which Joel had prophesied in which many would see visions, was inaugurated at Pentecost (Acts 2:16). Peter himself was emboldened by a vision to break with centuries of cultural and legal heritage to commence and to continue to minister to non-Jews (Acts 10:9-23; 11:5).

The Apostle Paul's conversion and call were through a dramatic vision (Acts 9:1-9). His missionary focus was redirected from Asia to Europe by means of a vision (Acts 16:8). Via vision he received instruction to continue preaching at Corinth in spite of the risk of increased personal danger (Acts 18:9).

Our knowledge of future events, scant though it is, is mostly dependent upon another vision, that given to the Apostle John while he was exiled on the island of Patmos (Revelation 1:9-19).

From Genesis to Revelation, there is the record of God speaking, instructing and directing his people through visions conveyed in various ways. So why might it be so difficult or rare for his people today similarly to receive such?

WE'RE NOT CALLED TO LIVE BY HUMAN REASON. ALL THAT MATTERS IS OBEDIENCE TO GOD'S WORD AND HIS LEADING IN OUR LIVES ... WHEN WE ARE IN HIS WILL, WE ARE IN THE SAFEST PLACE IN THE WORLD.

Perhaps it has to do somewhat with faith and courage. We know that without faith it is impossible to please God (Hebrews 11:6). We say we have it, at least for salvation. But in the modern western welfare state, which compensates for most of life's emergencies and cocoons us in its embrace from cradle to grave, who needs more? Could it be that we enter our churches and attend our conferences, sing our songs and make our speeches saying we have faith in God, but then so organise our personal affairs as to be in practice no different from atheists? Faith which the Bible teaches and exemplifies would not be just talking about diamonds, but expecting to find them on our doorsteps.

It would not be talking of making butter out of milk, but doing that when no cows exist!

Perhaps for these reasons, vision may be so rare in our church life at all levels. Conversely for these same reasons God may today be raising up the greatest church in the history of the world. As one of its leaders typically wrote,

"We're not called to live by human reason. All that matters is obedience to God's word and his leading in our lives. If God says go we'll go. If he says stay we'll stay. When we are in his will, we are in the safest place in the world."

With that widespread attitude, it's not surprising that vision is commoner in the emerging church of China. It knows that in spite of all the continued risks and hardships associated with being a believer under an aggressively atheistic Communist regime, the church that lives for itself dies by itself. They, like Benedict, Francis of Assisi, Francis Xavier, De Nobili, Tyndale, Carey, Judson, Wilberforce and a host of other historical visionaries, have received their own vision from God. In spite of all the obstacles, they will not live protectively for themselves. They intend to take the message of Jesus back to Jerusalem and beyond.

FOUR

WHY VISION?

In typically memorable lines, the Bible succinctly sums up the need for vision. In classical expression it states,

"Where there is no vision, the people perish" (Proverbs 29:18 KJV).

Finding nothing better to live for, people cease worshipping God and start worshipping other entities, even themselves. Without fresh revelation people do whatever is right in their own eyes. There is little to keep them on their toes in expectancy or to drive them to their knees in dependency upon God. They may boast about the Lord but so control events as to never have to put him to the test. The deplorable becomes inevitable as it is presented as acceptable and becomes desirable.

Such was precisely the case at Shiloh, with the ministering priests in general and Eli's sons in particular (1 Samuel 2:12-22). Whether because of wide spread sin or because no corrective action was taken, the fact remained that, *"in those days the word of the Lord was rare; there were not many visions."* (1 Samuel 3:1).

Similarly today, without vision we will be prone to repeat the past, drifting aimlessly, following fads, settling for the commonest second or third best, doing and accepting whatever the majority of people embrace, with little to distinguish us from everyone else as God's supposedly unique people.

Without vision we will settle for what is, rather than what should be. Without vision we will be reluctant or afraid to take leaps of faith, forgetting that chasms can't be crossed in a series of small controlled steps.

Without vision we may have no goals for the future, or if we do, they would hardly qualify for that description. As Michelangelo once said, "The greater danger for most of us is not that our aim is too high and we miss it, but that it is too low and we reach it."

Centuries ago a small band of brave pilgrims in search of religious freedom left Europe and sailed to the shores of what today is known as the United States of America. With great vision and courage they went forth to settle in the New World.

In their first year these historic immigrants established a town which became known as Plymouth, Massachusetts. In their second year they elected a council to manage the affairs of the settlement. In the third year, that council proposed building a road 8 kilometres westward into unsettled territory. But in the fourth year the people tried to impeach the town council because they thought a road into the forest was a waste of money.

Somehow these forward looking visionaries, who to achieve their vision had risked their lives by leaving Europe and sailing across 5000 kilometres of ocean, had unaccountably lost all sense of vision. They could not see the need to commence to go west to explore the vast continent before them with all of its wealth waiting to be discovered.

But their attitude was not unprecedented. The ancient Israelites were similarly disposed. General Joshua led them in several stunning military victories, but with time they settled for treaties and compromise rather than pushing on to possess all which God had reserved for them (Judges1:19-36). The effects of that are still being felt to this day.

Christians in every age are not too dissimilar. We start out with such marvellous hopes, visions, dreams, determination, discipline and diligence. We are motivated by God's Word and the Holy Spirit. After a few blessings and instances of answered prayer we start to congratulate ourselves, live life by looking into the rear vision mirrors of our experience and settle into security, satisfaction and contentment. We gradually lose our sense of urgency and high calling toward our destiny in God.

Maybe Michelangelo was such an outstandingly commanding figure of history because he once prayed: "Lord, grant that I may always desire more than I can accomplish."

That attitude kept him moving forward in his chosen fields as a very high achiever. So what may vision do for us?

FIVE

WHAT VISION DOES

Firstly vision enables us to "see".

Helen Keller, who was speech, hearing and sight impaired said that the only thing worse than being blind was to have eyesight but no vision. Vision is not dependent upon physical eyesight. Jonathan Swift defined it as the art of seeing the invisible.

United States President John F. Kennedy said, "The problems of the world cannot be solved by sceptics or cynics whose horizons are limited by obvious realities. We need (people) who can dream of things that never were."

Kennedy exemplified that by challenging his nation to go where none had previously gone, to create a path which others could follow and to put a man on the moon by the end of the decade of the 1960s. He understood intuitively something which communist agitator Douglas Hyde, used to teach his team leaders before he converted to Christianity:

"If you make mean little demands on people, you'll get mean, little responses; if you make heroic demands, you'll get heroic responses."

At huge cost to the nation in terms of money, man power, resources and lives Kennedy's vision pulled reality toward it, rather than the reverse which more frequently happens.

SPIRITUAL LEADERS ARE THOSE WHO SEE MORE THAN OTHERS SEE, WHO SEE FURTHER THAN OTHERS SEE AND WHO SEE LONGER THAN OTHERS SEE.

In the 1992 United States Presidential elections, candidate Clinton emphasised vision. President Bush (snr) discounted it. Although reasons for election outcomes are usually complex, future candidates understood that they would ignore the vision factor, to their own peril.

Former national director for Overseas Missionary Fellowship (OMF) in Australia, Allan Webb, says spiritual leaders are those who see more than others see, who see further than others see and who see longer than others see. This enables them to see the future as present, the invisible as seen and the impossible as done.

Viennese psychiatrist Victor Frankl was incarcerated in a Nazi concentration camp during the Second World War. After the war he addressed his fellow Austrians as follows:

There is only one reason why I am here today and it is you. What kept me alive was you. Others gave up hope. I dreamed. I dreamed that someday I would be telling you that I, Victor Frankl had survived the Nazi concentration camps. I've never been here before. I've never seen any of you before. I've never given this speech before. But in my dreams I have stood before you and said these words a thousand times.

That "sight" saved his life.

Secondly, vision enables us to focus on the future.

Vision helps us to see the present through future glasses. It helps us to challenge the present to create opportunities for the future. With vision we are able to draw a picture of what we would like to become, what we should become, what we will become by God's grace and enabling.

> WE NEED TO BE VISION GUIDED RATHER THAN HISTORY HAMPERED. THERE IS LITTLE FUTURE IN LIVING IN THE PAST.

When Australian Christian businessman Roger Corbett met American Sam Walton the founder of Walmart, one of the world's most successful companies, Corbett was impacted by Walton's focus, commitment and determination to build an even greater company in the future. Corbett started as a labourer unloading trucks for Woolworths, Australia. Along the way, inspired by what he had learned, he went on to become that same company's CEO and built it into the leading supermarket chain in Australia.

Additionally Corbett demonstrated that we should never allow the past to enter the present to dictate the future. It is especially important to remember that if Jesus forgives and forgets the past, where necessary so should we. We are going to live the rest of our lives in the future so that's where our focus needs to be. We need to be vision guided rather than history hampered.

There is little future in living in the past. But judging by the waiting lists for Christian counselling centres one might conclude that it's easier for God to keep us out of trouble than to get us out of trouble. People of vision do not live lives clouded by distress, despair or disillusionment, pulled backward focussing on past problems. Vision takes their eyes off themselves and focuses them on the future and God, who is already waiting there to meet them when they arrive.

In Ho Chi Minh City there is a restaurant called "Yesterday". But if one looks carefully at the menu, the Vietnamese reads as "Ngay Mai" which translates as "Tomorrow". When the proprietor was asked to explain he replied: "You foreigners are always talking about yesterday. You say, 'Do you remember when…?' Here in Vietnam people have forgotten about yesterday. The only thing we care about is tomorrow."

Playwright George Bernard Shaw once said, "Some people see things and ask, 'Why'. But I dream of things that never were and say, 'Why not?'" Why not indeed. Unfortunately too many of us are pinioned to our past rather than focussed on the future.

When Los Angeles police officers noticed an immaculately restored vintage car being driven erratically, they moved immediately to pull the driver over to the side of the road. They assumed he was over the alcohol limit for safe driving. They were surprised to learn that the driver was a

> UNLESS THERE IS AN ELEMENT OF RISK IN OUR EXPLOITS FOR GOD THERE IS NO NEED FOR FAITH.

gadget enthusiast. He had attached no fewer than 18 rear vision mirrors to his vehicle. He was so engrossed viewing where he had been with the help of his rear vision mirrors, that he wasn't focussed on where he was going.

The lesson is so obvious for leaders and church it hardly needs drawing out.

Thirdly, vision gives us faith to believe.

"Faith is being sure of what we hope for and certain of what we do not see" (Hebrews 11:1).

Vision helps us to see the invisible, hear the inaudible, think the unthinkable, believe the incredible and do the impossible.

A shoe manufacturer wanting to open up the largely undeveloped market for his product in the Central African Republic of the Congo, sent two salesmen to survey for possibilities. One messaged him saying, "Prospect here nil. No one wears shoes." The other reported, "Market potential terrific. Everyone is barefooted."

It's obvious only one of them would understand the power of what Greek orator Demosthenes said a few millennia earlier. "Small opportunities are often the beginning of great enterprises."

Many people are risk averse. They like to live well within safe borders without challenging the outer limits. Hudson Taylor, founder of what today is known as Overseas Missionary Fellowship (OMF) was not one of them. He said that "unless there is an element of risk in our exploits for God there is no need for faith." He lived accordingly. The person who risks nothing, may find at the end of their life they have achieved nothing of significance in God.

If we are to find good fruit, we have to go out on a limb. At least out there the view will be better. Only in response to vision can we set huge,

God honouring, faith dependent stretch goals. In so doing, we need to remember that in cooperating with God to build his church, it's more akin to growing oak trees than mushrooms. A mushroom matures in 12 hours. An oak takes 60-100 years.

When God gave Abraham, aged 75, a vision (Genesis 12:1-3), it sustained him to remember what only God could do (Romans 4:17). It enabled him to rely on God's promises (Romans 4:18). It helped him to recognise the facts of faith (Romans 4:19-20a) and relax to rejoice in anticipation of the surety that God would do exactly what he said he would do (Romans 4:20-21). What is impossible with men is possible with God (Luke 18:27). That promise certainly gives us faith to believe for even greater things from God.

Fourthly, vision releases the courage to act.

It is well said that there are three sorts of people:

1. Those who make things happen.

2. Those who watch things happen.

3. Those who wonder what happened.

Many people decline action for fear of failure. The problem with that is we are doomed if we don't even try. That could not be said of one of the world's great twentieth century visionaries – William Booth, the founder and first General of the Salvation Army. Once God gave him a vision of people lost without Jesus and the awesome import of what that meant for both here and eternity, nothing could stop him except his own death. When that happened it resulted in the greatest funeral England had ever seen. Booth commanded his troops to "charge on the hosts of hell and see whether they will not turn and flee." He led that charge from the front.

In the physical realm there were abundant precedents for what would otherwise be regarded as recklessness. In World War One the battle of the Marne was critical if France was to survive. French Army commander

> THE BRAVEST ARE SURELY THOSE WHO HAVE THE CLEAREST VISION OF WHAT IS BEFORE THEM, GLORY AND DANGER ALIKE AND YET NOTWITHSTANDING GO OUT TO MEET IT.

General Foch knew he faced a very dangerous situation. He knew all he had at his disposal was a thin line of troops between the advancing Germans and Paris. If Paris was lost that would be the end of everything. Having listened to the reports from all his staff officers he issued his orders: "My right is defeated. My left is broken. I attack."

He exemplified what Greek historian Thucydides concluded many centuries previously:

The bravest are surely those who have the clearest vision of what is before them, glory and danger alike and yet notwithstanding go out to meet it.

In 1991 Mikhail Gorbachev and Boris Yeltsin nurtured a vision of a vastly different Russia from what had preceded it during seven decades of Communist government. But some Russian Generals, determined to stem the growing tide of democracy, placed Gorbachev under house arrest at his dacha outside of Moscow. Tanks rumbled into Red Square to capture second-in-command, Boris Yeltsin. But Yeltsin, fired by his vision of a new Russia, took extraordinary action. Instead of meekly surrendering as had entire populations confronted with Communism wielding power out of the barrel of a gun, he leaped onto the leading tank and welcomed its commander over to his side of democracy. Later that army officer confessed he came with no intention of joining the forces of democracy, but Yeltsin was so persuasive he was irresistible. Yeltsin's single bold action signalled the end of Communism's power in Russia.

Lech Walesa, the Gdansk shipyard electrician acted with similar courage and vision to defeat Communism in Poland.

Rosa Parks, an African American woman living in Montgomery, Alabama, refused to sit in the back of a bus because of the colour of her skin. Martin Luther King later said that her single act spurred him into action to build the civil rights movement whose vision was to abolish legalised racial discrimination in the USA.

Nelson Mandela's decades of imprisonment on Robin Island similarly contributed to the demolition of apartheid in South Africa.

In Puyang County, north east Henan, in China, local people ridiculed Mennonite missionary Henry Brown, when in 1917 he constructed what for the time was a huge 700 seat building. Few citizens showed a little interest in the gospel Brown preached. His vision and construction was mostly compared to the foolishness of Noah building the ark.

When the Communists took over in 1950, the church was confiscated and used as a warehouse. In 1993 it was returned to the Christian community. After restoration was completed, the church was officially opened in October 1994. More than 1000 people crammed into the building with many more standing in the courtyard outside. The church has continued to overflow with worshipers and seekers ever since. The effects of authentic vision often outlast the visionary.

For someone implementing God's vision, at first it often seems impossible. Then it is seen as difficult, till finally it is done.

SIX

HOW TO GET VISION

As the biographies of countless Christian visionaries confirm, vision always begins with dissatisfaction with the status quo, a longing for things to be different with better and more effective outcomes. Visionaries understand that if their lives and ministries are to make a significant difference, they need to interact with the mind and heart of God. Therefore they:

> VISIONARIES UNDERSTAND THAT IF THEIR LIVES AND MINISTRIES ARE TO MAKE A SIGNIFICANT DIFFERENCE, THEY NEED TO INTERACT WITH THE MIND AND HEART OF GOD.

» Immerse themselves in the Word of God.

» Give themselves to extraordinary prayer expectantly waiting upon God.

» Carefully survey and analyse the needs and options of the environment in which they are situated.

The ministries of Joshua, Ezra and Nehemiah all demonstrate these simple principles. The process is unchanged. As a young Youth With A Mission (YWAM) worker, Floyd McClung spent many hours walking the streets of Amsterdam. He was looking at the people, discerning their needs and praying for God to reveal to him how best to tie the strands together. Once he knew the answer, he commenced a new ministry which had an impact far beyond Amsterdam.

People seeking God's vision for their particular mission, frequently follow a familiar path. What draws them through is the repeated evidences of God's presence, fortified by the appropriation of his word. The familiar dialogue of vision and its implementation could be as follows:

Visionary says, "It's impossible." God replies, *"All things are possible"* (Luke 18:27).

Visionary, "I can't do it." God, *"You can do all things through Christ"* (Philippians 4:13).

Visionary, "I'm not able." God, *"I am able"* (2 Corinthians 9:8).

Visionary, "I'm afraid." God, *"I have not given you a spirit of fear"* (2 Timothy 1:7).

Visionary, "I don't have enough faith." God, *"I've given everyone a measure of faith"* (Romans 12:3).

Visionary, "I'm not smart enough." God, *" I will give you wisdom"* (1 Corinthians 1:30).

Visionary, "But I can't figure it out." God, *"I'll direct your steps"* (Proverbs 3:5-6).

Visionary, "I'll not be able to manage." God, *"I'll supply all your needs"* (Philippians 4:19).

Visionary, "I'm too tired." God, *"I will give you rest"* (Matthew 11:28-30).

Visionary, "I can't go on." God, *"My grace is sufficient"* (2 Corinthians 12:9).

Visionary, "I feel all alone." God, *"I will never leave you or forsake you"* (Hebrews 13:5).

Visionary, "I'm so worried." God, *"Cast all your cares on me"* (1 Peter 5:7).

Visionary, "It's not worth it." God, *"It will be worth it"* (Romans 8:28).

We are commonly excellent at thinking up reasons for not acting or advancing. Fortunately God has heard it all before from Moses, Gideon, Isaiah, Jeremiah, Peter and many others. Yet he never gives up. Neither should we.

Having understood what God's vision may be, the next step is to write it down as succinctly as possible. (Habakkuk 2:2) To be memorable it should be distilled into one sentence in bumper sticker form. Then comes the tough part–communicating the vision and gaining acceptance.

Amazing growth in churches, and astounding changes in society, came about in part because for 40 years one man prayed and worked, seeing the establishment of thousands of similar meetings, all united in calling on God for revival.

Missionary societies were established. William Carey was one who got swept up in that movement. The environment of his situation was that he was a member of a ministers' revival prayer group which had been meeting for two years in Northampton in 1784-86. It was in 1786 he shared his vision of God's desire to see the heathen won for the Lord. He went on to establish what later became known as the Baptist Missionary Society. In 1795 the London Missionary Society was formed. In 1796 the Scottish Missionary Society was established and later still the Church Missionary Society of the Anglicans was commenced.

SEVEN

TELLING IT LIKE IT IS

Vision by itself accomplishes little. Between the conceptualizing of a vision and it becoming a reality lies much hard work. It's one thing to receive a vision of a "promised land." It's another to take possession. In between there may be many "wilderness" experiences. For Joseph, between the dream and the diadem there was the dungeon. It's these experiences which God uses to temper and remould his chosen vessels (Psalm 105:17-19). It's also these experiences which sort out true visionaries from mere dreamers.

Pastors who are managers busy themselves with analysis, problem solving and planning. Visionaries prioritize communication of vision and values to translate vision into reality and effect change.

Any church is a complex organism regardless of size. Just as the whole range of spiritual gifts are never entrusted to any single individual to oblige interdependency, so a pastor or spiritual leader is never invested with the multiplicity of office needed for the proper functioning of any church (Ephesians 4:11-16).

Visionaries need firstly to communicate with the body to whom organisational governance is entrusted. Only after the vision has been probed, prayed and confirmed by them should it be shared with the wider community. The pastor or team leader may not be the exclusive visionary but he needs to be the chief vision caster and guardian.

As vision enters the more public domain, the way forward may become more difficult,

> THE VISION CASTER NEEDS TO BE WELL PREPARED FOR THE COUNTER WAVE WHICH INEVITABLY COMES.

distressing, depressing or even dangerous. The vision bearer may risk popularity, peace and profession. About 15% of any group of people will be early adaptors, 15% will not adapt and 70% are persuadable either way. Non-adaptors will be able to influence some to their way of thinking.

The vision caster needs to be well prepared for the counter wave which inevitably comes. Moses, Ezra and Nehemiah all encountered it. It's unlikely ever to be different.

EIGHT

AGAINST THE TIDE

Isaac Newton's third law of motion states that to every reaction there is an equal and opposite reaction. This is a painful experience for Christian leaders who are also commanded to "make every effort to keep the unity of the Spirit through the bond of peace" (Ephesians 4:3). Any vision when first announced frequently results in reaction and conflict. The question then is which party succumbs first to fear. Fear is a common component even of God's greatest servants (Exodus 3:5-4:16; 1 Kings 19:3; Isaiah 6:5; Jeremiah 1:4-7; Revelation 1:17). Faith is the position to which God wants to nudge us. Courage isn't the absence of fear. It's moving forward in spite of fear.

Oswald Chambers once said, "God gives us a vision then takes us down to the valley to batter us into the shape of that vision and it is in the valley that so many of us faint and give way."

When we think we have received some new revelation from God, we become excited and often sprint into action. That's the folly of inexperience. On the plains of Africa, cheetahs survive by sprinting after their prey at up to 110 kilometres per hour. Unless they catch their prey within a few minutes, they abandon the chase. In their long, sleek bodies there are disproportionately small hearts, which cause them to tire quickly. But vision implementation is not for sprinters. The prize goes usually to marathon runners.

Revelation is "wow". This is "now" – which within the context of initial conflict, seems to stretch on for eternity.

When Moses went to implement his God given vision of leading out God's people from Egypt, firstly there was repeated resistance from Pharaoh (Exodus 5-12). That was understandable. But more difficult to endure was conflict repeatedly generated by the very people he was trying to help (Exodus 15:22-17:7).

When Joshua went to possess the "promised land", he had to battle for every bit of it and still didn't entirely succeed (Judges 1). When Ezra went to resettle Jerusalem and Nehemiah went to rebuild the walls (Ezra 4:1-5; Nehemiah 4), both confronted conflict.

In today's church, conflict results in few fatalities unless one factors in death through the effects of prolonged stress. Resistance is more polite but nevertheless resolute. For example, how often is it stated:

» We've tried that before.
» Has anyone else ever tried that?
» We don't have time and other resources.
» It will cost too much.
» Someone might object.
» Why change? Don't fix what isn't broken.
» We did all right without it.
» It won't work here.
» Let's give it some more thought.
» We've never done that before.
» What if….

When the dust settles and the new vision starts to come into effect, review of the process often reveals a familiar pattern. Firstly the vision is disregarded by many as "nonsense". Then it is "too expensive" to consider. Next it becomes a "good idea". Finally an argument may break out as to "who thought of it first"!

What is required to overcome resistance is persistence. As a Chinese proverb says, "Be not afraid of moving slowly. Be afraid only of standing still."

NINE

WALKING THE TALK

If we believe God has given us a vision, then we must believe he has predestined us to prevail. Michelangelo kept pounding and painting regardless of opposition and setbacks. Martin Luther declined to recant when most of the church hierarchy opposed him.

Thomas Edison did not give up on his efforts to invent an incandescent light bulb, in spite of thousands of failed attempts and his own assistants' serious doubts. During the darkest days of World War II, even in retreat, General Douglas Macarthur announced to the defeated American and Philippines army units, "I shall return."

They all prevailed.

As former University of Alabama famed football coach, Bear Bryant used to tell his team, "What matters is not the size of the dog in the fight but the size of the fight in the dog."

Ray Kroc, founder of McDonalds, said to his staff:

Press on. Nothing in the world can take the place of persistence. Talent will not; nothing is more common than unsuccessful talented individuals. Genius will not. The world is full of educated derelicts. Persistence and determination alone count... When others quit and give up...keep working.

Persistence pays.

"Do not throw away your confidence; it will be richly rewarded. You need to persevere so that when you have done the will of God, you will receive what he has promised" (Hebrews 11:35-36).

In 1893 Walter Gowans, Rowland Bingham and Tom Kent arrived in Lagos, Nigeria fired with a vision to plant churches among the 60 million unreached people who then inhabited Africa's 4000 kilometre wide interior known as the Soudan. As they journeyed they were told, "You will never see the Soudan. Your children will never see the Soudan. Your grandchildren may." All three became infected with malaria. Gowans and Kent soon died but their vision lived on.

In 1901 a mission station was established at Patigi, Nigeria. Others prayed, gave and went, till an effective barrier was built against the further spread southwards of early 20th century Islam. The mission became known as Soudan Interior Mission which evolved into SIM International, one of the largest non-denominational missionary agencies in the world today.

If God gives a vision, he will also give the strength and the resources to endure till it becomes reality. Always remember, that in the struggle between a stream and a rock, the stream wins – not through strength or force, but by persistence.

TEN

THE END OF THE BEGINNING

The original "daring young man on the flying trapeze" was a Frenchman named Jules Leotard. On November 12, 1859 he made circus history at the Cirque Napoleon de Paris. Launching from a fixed platform he swung out holding on to a trapeze bar. At the top of his swing he let go of the bar and floated unsupported through the air for 5 metres. He then reached out and grabbed

> VISIONARIES ARE COURAGEOUS ENOUGH TO LET GO, TO REACH OUT TO OPPORTUNITIES JUST BEYOND THEIR GRASP.

another trapeze bar swinging toward him. The crowd went wild. No trapeze artist before Leotard had ever completely released a hold on the first bar before grabbing the second.

Visionaries are courageous enough to let go, to reach out to opportunities just beyond their grasp. Unless one releases the old, the new will never be grasped.

In the first century of the Christian era, what was thought to be a small religious sect, emerged with a dynamic message which offered an unprecedented alternative as to how people should live. In spite of fearsome opposition and many failings, they dramatically jostled their way through competing ideologies and overcame many obstacles. The church had arrived led by visionaries who "turned the world upside down" (Acts 17:6).

Throughout history, leaders have emerged who were convinced they had received a vision from God, and proceeded to make their contribution to making a difference to the world of their day.

IT'S NEVER THE MINISTRY, MONEY, METHOD OR OTHER PEOPLE WHICH MATTER FOR ETERNITY. IT'S ONLY GOD.

Now it is our turn, to march to the beat of another drum, in step with the Infinite, empowered by the Spirit, as the people of God for our generation. Whatever vision God gives you, seek confirmation and implement it with persistence. Whatever difference you make, end as you began, by giving God the glory. It's never the ministry, money, method or other people which matter for eternity. It's only God.

ELEVEN

A PERSONAL WORD

In 1965 God dramatically called me from what I thought was my work for him in Australia. His assignment for me was to relocate to South Asia, to live and work among a people who historically had been most resistant to the Christian message. For a couple of centuries, in spite of many attempts, the response from among these people was almost zero.

Years had to be spent learning about the religious and cultural background of these people – as well as their language. Eventually circumstances allowed me to focus full time on the task, almost without distraction of other responsibilities. After more years of prayer and study of God's Word and of the people we were to reach, completely new methodologies were developed, in cooperation with a few other workers. These proved amazingly effective, but were opposed by many church and mission leaders. God gave a vision of seeing some thousands of these difficult to reach people grafted into his kingdom. That figure was passed long ago. The methodologies which were so resisted have since been adapted and adopted in many other countries, with similar results.

In 1982 God suddenly called me back to Australia, to pastor a church. I knew little of how to carry out the new assignment. As I studied the context of this new ministry, in my first year God gave a vision of what he wanted this church to become. I would happily have died at that point realising the implications of what was involved – principally reorganising, relocating, rebuilding and lots of money.

It took several years to have the vision confirmed and accepted by the church. The effect of the new direction caused conflict and many left.

> WITH TIME, ACCORDING TO GOD'S VISION, THE IMPOSSIBLE BECOMES POSSIBLE AND THE FUTURE REMAINS AS BRIGHT AS HIS PROMISES.

Today the new church, Crossway, existing on 6 hectares of land and at 2 other sites in suburban Melbourne, has grown continuously since its relocation eleven years ago. Today there are 4000 people in weekend attendance. In the last decade it has planted 10 other congregations and supports 56 of its members in cross-cultural mission. It owes no debt on its $20m. facility and is preparing major extensions to accommodate continuous growth.

By experience we have learned that "faith" is spelt R-I-S-K. We define it as walking in the midst of miracles always on the edge of disaster. Our desire is to be guided by God into something so big, it is doomed to failure unless God is in it.

With time, according to God's vision, the impossible becomes possible and the future remains as bright as his promises.

About The Author

Stuart Robinson is the Founding Pastor of Australia's largest Baptist Church. Before that he worked for fourteen years in South Asia where he pioneered church planting among Muslims. He travels extensively as a speaker at Conferences. He is the author of eight books including the best-selling titles, *Mosques & Miracles*, *Defying Death* and *The Prayer of Obedience.* He graduated from four tertiary institutions. Stuart was born in Brisbane and is married to Margaret. They have three married children.

By the same author

Traveling Through Troubled Times

Mosques & Miracles: Revealing Islam and God's Grace

Defying Death: Zakaria Botross — Apostle to Islam

The Challenge of Islam

Growing Your Church Supernaturally: Persevering Prayer

Positioning For Power

Praying The Price

You can purchase these titles from:

www.amazon.com

www.bookdepository.co.uk

www.koorong.com

www.chibooks.org

www.ingramcontent.com/pod-product-compliance
Lightning Source LLC
Chambersburg PA
CBHW060042040426
42331CB00032B/2238